Mother Earth: My Favourite Artist Lesson Plan
Created by Nadine Ottenbreit (Métis)
Approved by Author: Carol Rose GoldenEagle
April 1st, 2025
ISBN: 978-1-77854-0622

$7.99 CAD / $5.95 USD

ISBN 978-1-77854-062-2
50595>
9 781778 540622

Welcome

Welcome to our exciting journey into the world of nature and art! In the following lessons, we will discover the wonders of Mother Earth and how she is the greatest artist of all. From the vibrant colours of flowers, and the unique patterns of animal tracks to the insects that help flowers grow, nature is full of incredible things that can inspire us every day. In these lessons, we will discover how it is important to take care of our planet and how we can show our love for Mother Earth through art. Art helps children to:

- Express Themselves: Art is a way for children to express their ideas, feelings, and thoughts in a unique way.
- Foster Imagination: Art helps children use their creativity and produce innovative ideas.
- Develop Fine Motor Skills: Painting, drawing, textile, collages, and sculpting are activities that enhance children's control and co-ordination of their hands and eyes.
- Enhance Observation: Making art with nature helps children focus on the details and appreciate the world around them.
- Build Confidence: Children feel pride in themselves when they finish a project and gain a sense of accomplishment.

Contents

Activity 1

Mother Earth and Recycled Materials

Objective:

- To introduce children to the concept of Mother Earth and the importance of taking care of our planet.
- To encourage creativity and self-expression through art.

Materials Needed:

- Storybook Mother Earth: My Favourite Artist by Carol Rose GoldenEagle & Hawlii Pichette
- Large sheets of cardstock paper or poster boards (Using thicker paper will better support the glue and materials, making the project sturdier and less flimsy).
- Crayons, markers, or pencil crayons
- Glue and scissors
- Recycled materials (bottle caps, cardboard, paper scraps, toilet paper rolls)
- Nature items (leaves, twigs, flowers, rocks)

1. **Introduction:**

- **Discussion**: Briefly talk about what Mother Earth means. Explain that Mother Earth is another name for our planet and that it provides us with everything we need to live, like air, water, and food.

2. **Story Time:**

- **Read Aloud**: Read Mother Earth: My Favourite Artist by Carol Rose GoldenEagle & Hawlii Pichette. Point out the illustrations and ask questions to engage the children (Example: “What do you see in this picture?” “Have you seen animal tracks before? Where? What kind?” “Have you ever come across an interesting rock and decided to keep it?”).

3. **Nature Collage:**

- **Activity**: Children will create a collage using recycled materials and items from nature to show how beautiful Mother Earth is.

- **Create the Collage**: Provide each child with a large sheet of cardstock paper or poster board. Let them use crayons, markers, or coloured pencils to draw a background. Then, glue on recycled materials and nature items to create their collage. Encourage children to use their imagination and express their ideas about Mother Earth through their art just like she did in the story.

4. **Sharing and Reflection (optional):**

- **Show and Tell**: Allow each child to share their collage with the group. Ask them to explain what they created and why they chose certain materials.

5. **Closing:**

- **Discussion and Wrap-Up**: Talk about the importance of taking care of Mother Earth and how everyone can help, even in small ways (recycling, planting trees, saving water).

Activity 2

Discovering Animal Tracks

Objective:

- To introduce children to the concept of animal tracks and how to identify them.
- To encourage outdoor exploration and observation skills.

Materials Needed:

- Images of common animal tracks found in and around your community, including those of deer, rabbit, fox, squirrel, and geese. There are numerous free templates available online to help you decide which specific tracks you would like to include (to extend you can have them match the animal to their tracks.)
- Laminated tracks for students to create their own on top (or place the printed sheet in a plastic sleeve)
- Large sheets of paper
- Crayons, markers, or pencil crayons
- Clay or play dough
- Magnifying glasses (optional)
- Extend activity to cut the shape of deer hoof prints into a potato to create a stamp where they can make their own tracks.

1. **Introduction:**

- Discussion: Briefly talk about what animal tracks are and why they are important. Explain that animal tracks can tell us a lot about the animals that live in our area and their behaviours. Finding tracks also helps people find edible plants and helps hunters catch animals for food.

2. **Story Time:**

- Read Aloud: Read Mother Earth: My Favourite Artist by Carol Rose GoldenEagle & Hawlii Pichette. Point out the illustrations and ask questions to engage the children. To extend the activity you can also show short videos found online about animals and their tracks beforehand.

3. **Outdoor Exploration:**

- Track Hunt: Choose a safe, nearby location where animal tracks are likely to be found, such as a park or nature trail. Guide the children in searching for and identifying a variety of animal tracks. Use magnifying glasses for a closer look.

4. **Making Animal Tracks:**

- Create the Tracks: Provide each child with a piece of clay or playdough and show them how to press their fingers or small objects into it to create different animal tracks. Use pictures of common animal tracks as a reference. Let children experiment with making different tracks and patterns of their own.

5. **Sharing and Reflection (optional):**

- Show and Tell: Allow each child to share their clay tracks and any drawings they made during the track hunt.

6. **Closing:**

- Discussion and Wrap-Up: Talk about the different tracks they found and what they learned about the animals in their area.

Activity 3

Rock Painting

Objective:

- Students will learn ways to be creative and show self expression through their art.

Materials Needed:

- Clean, smooth rocks
- Acrylic paint
- Paintbrushes of various sizes, sponges
- Paint tray or paper plates
- Paint shirts
- Water cups for cleaning brushes
- Paper towel
- Sealant spray (optional)

1. **Introduction:**

- **Discussion**: Explain to students that they will be turning their ordinary rocks into art and that rock painting is one of the first ways that people were able to share their creativity.

2. **Story Time:**

- **Read Aloud**: Read Mother Earth: My Favourite Artist by Carol Rose GoldenEagle & Hawlii Pichette. Point out the illustrations and ask questions. “Have you ever found a unique rock before?” “Have you ever found a rock that looked like something else?” Discuss how all rocks are unique and that none are the same.

- **Examples**: Provide examples to inspire students. Discuss the variety of themes they can use to paint such as patterns, animal tracks, things found in nature, or abstract designs.

3. **Preparation:**

- **Design Planning**: Have students select their rocks and plan their designs on paper before painting.

- **Painting**: Start with a white base coat. Once it's dry, they can use a pencil to draw the outline of their picture if they like or they can paint freely.

- **Drying**: Allow the painted rocks to dry. Once completely dry the sealant spray may be used (optional).

4. **Show and Tell:**

- Have students share their painted rocks with the class and explain their designs.

- Variations: You could create a rock garden or introduce a talking circle using their painted rocks.

Activity 4

Pollination Game

Objective:

- To teach children about the role of ladybugs in pollination through a fun and interactive game.

Materials Needed:

- Pictures or cutouts of flowers and ladybugs
- Velcro dots or magnets
- Pompoms
- A large board or wall space
- Small baskets or containers

Setup:

1. Prepare the Flowers and Ladybugs: Print or draw pictures of different flowers and ladybugs. Attach Velcro dots or magnets to the back of each picture and pompom.

2. Create the Pollination Station: Set up either a large board, white board or use a wall space where you can stick the flower and bee pictures. Arrange the flowers on one side and place the ladybugs and pompoms in small baskets or containers nearby.

How to Play:

1. Introduction: Read page 13 of *Mother Earth: My Favourite Artist* (note: there is a typo, "followers" should be "flowers"). Explain that pollination takes place when ladybugs help flowers grow by carrying pollen from one flower to another. Discuss why pollination is important. The artist has painted ladybugs, are there other bugs that pollinate?

2. Game Instructions:

- Each child takes turns picking a ladybug from the basket.
- The child then "flies" the ladybug to a flower and sticks it onto the board next to the flower.
- Encourage the children to make buzzing sounds and pretend to be ladybugs as they move around.

Variations:

- **Color Matching**: Use flowers and ladybugs of assorted colours and ask the children to match the ladybugs to the flowers of the same color.
- **Counting Game**: Number the flowers and ladybugs and have the children match them by numbers to practice counting skills.
- **Pompom Pollination:** Use pompoms as pollen that the ladybugs carry from flower to flower to pollinate them.

3. **Discussion**: After all the ladybugs have been matched with flowers, talk about how ladybugs help flowers grow and why pollination is important.

Activity 5

Free Creation with Open-Ended Materials

Objective:

- To encourage children to explore their creativity and imagination through open-ended materials.
- To offer a space where children can express their creativity without direct instruction from teachers.

Materials Needed:

1. Art supplies (crayons, markers, pencil crayons, paint)
2. Craft supplies (scissors, glue, tape)
3. Natural items (leaves, rocks, acorns, pinecones, sticks)
4. Recycled materials (toilet paper or paper towel rolls, cardboard, bottle caps, paper scraps, string/yarn, popsicle sticks, buttons, egg cartons, scrap fabric pieces)

Setup:

1. **Create an Invitation to Play:**

- Arrange materials in an inviting way on tables or in different stations around the classroom or outside.
- Ensure that the materials are organized and allow for easy access and exploration by the children.

2. **Introduction:**

- **Discussion or Circle Time**: Explain that they will get to create anything they want using the materials provided. Remind them that there is no right or wrong way to use the materials and to use their imagination.

3. **Free Creation Time:**

- **Observe and Support**: Teachers should observe the children's creations and provide support only when needed. Encourage children to share their ideas and to collaborate with each other.

- **Promote Independence:** Allow children to move freely between the different stations and choose the materials they want to use. Remind them that they are in charge of their creations and that they can change or add to their creations as they wish.

4. **Sharing and Reflection:**

- **Show and Tell:** Allow children to share their creation with each other and with you. Ask them to explain what they made.

Activity 6

Fill in the Blank

Fill in the best answer for each question.

Word Box		
frozen	Artist	greeted
Muskwa	game	treasure

1. Mother Earth: My Favourite ______________________________.

2. Each day, I am ______________________________ by the beauty of her pallet.

3. Sometimes when I'm out on the Land, I think she's inspiring me to play a

______________________________.

4. I do find ______________________________...in the form of a heart-shaped rock.

5. I see the image of a fish outlined in the ice of a __________________________ lake.

6. I can't help but paint one more picture. My favourite animal: The brown bear,

__________________________ in Cree.

Activity 7

How Can We Protect Mother Earth: Word Web

Name: ____________________________

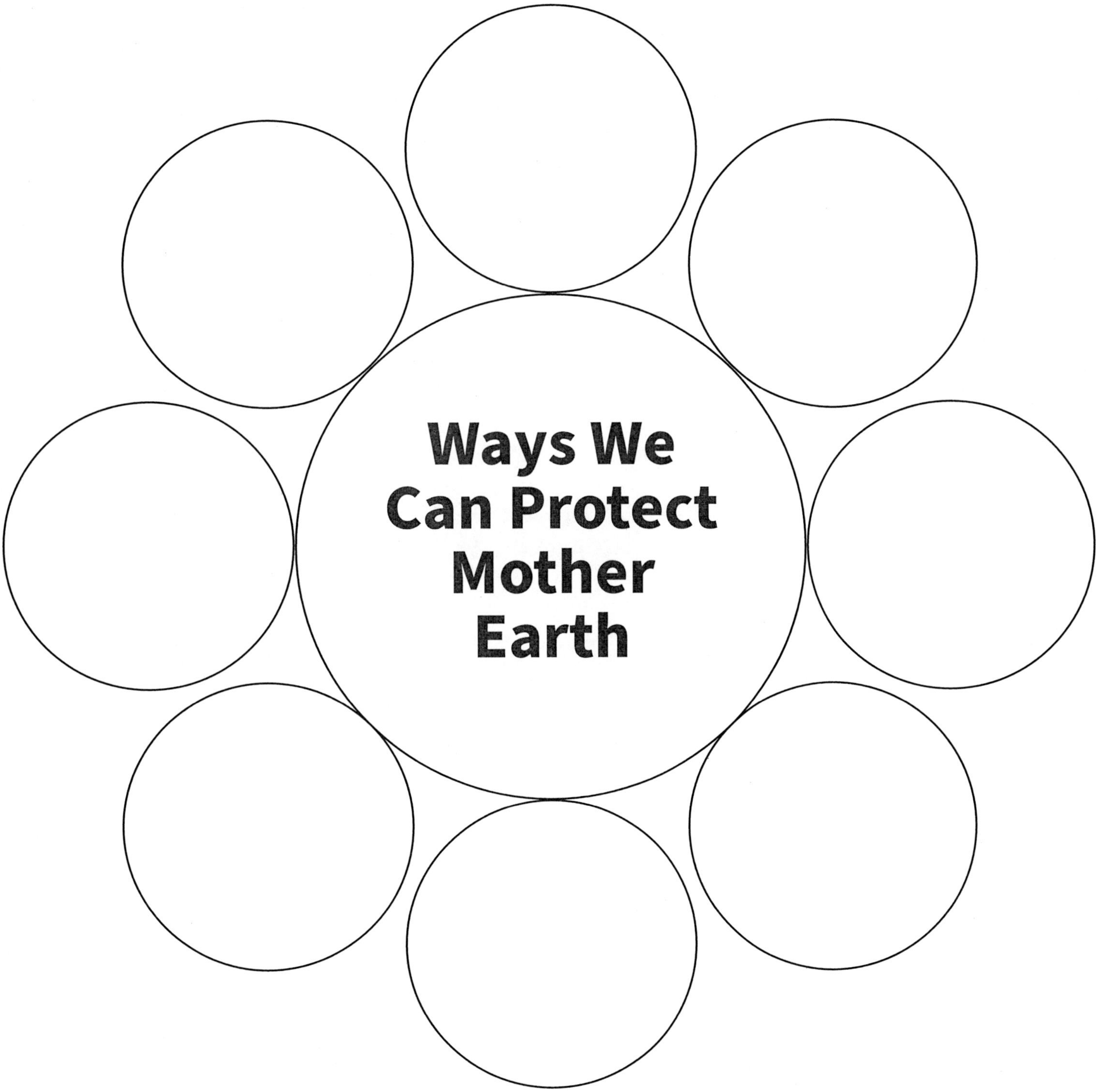

Activity 8

Colouring Pages